M000310231

Life Under the Sea

Sea Turtles

by Cari Meister

Ideas for Parents and Teachers

Bullfrog Books let children practice reading informational text at the earliest reading levels. Repetition, familiar words, and photo labels support early readers.

Before Reading

- Ask the child to think about sea turtles. Ask: What do you know about sea turtles?
- Look at the picture glossary together. Read and discuss the words.

Read the Book

- Read the book to the child, or have him or her read independently.
- Point out the photo labels to reinforce new vocabulary as you read.

After Reading

- Prompt the child to think more. Ask: Which body parts help sea turtles swim? Do you think sea turtles move faster on land or in water?

Bullfrog Books are published by Jump!
5357 Penn Avenue South
Minneapolis, MN 55419
www.jumplibrary.com

Library of Congress Cataloging-in-
Meister, Cari.
  Sea turtles / by Cari Meister.
     p. cm. -- (Bullfrog books. Life under the sea)
  Summary: "This photo-illustrated book for early readers tells the story of a sea turtle laying her eggs, how they hatch, find their way to the sea, and grow up"-- Provided by publisher.
  Audience: 005.
  Audience: K to grade 3.
  Includes bibliographical references and index.
  ISBN 978-1-62031-034-2 (hardcover : alk. paper) --
ISBN 978-1-62496-052-9 (ebook)
  1. Sea turtles--Juvenile literature. 2. Sea turtles--Behavior--Juvenile literature. I. Title.
  QL666.C536M443 2014
  597.92'8--dc23   2013001960

Series Editor   Rebecca Glaser
Book Designer   Ellen Huber
Photo Researcher Heather Dreisbach

Photo Credits: Alamy, 8, 12, 20, 23tr; Getty, 1, 14-15, 16-17; iStockPhoto, 4; Shutterstock, cover, 3t, 3b, 5, 9, 21, 22, 23tl, 23bl, 23br, 24; SuperStock, 13, 19; Veer, 6-7, 10-11, 18

Printed in the United States of America at Corporate Graphics, North Mankato, Minnesota.
5-2013 / PO 1003

10 9 8 7 6 5 4 3 2 1

Table of Contents

Making a Nest

It is night.

A sea turtle swims to shore.

5

It is time to lay her eggs.

Her front flippers
clear a spot.

front
flipper

Her hind flippers
dig a hole.

8

She lays her eggs.
She covers them
with sand.

hind
flipper

9

Then, she swims away.

She will never see her babies.

In time, the eggs hatch.

The hatchlings hurry to the water.

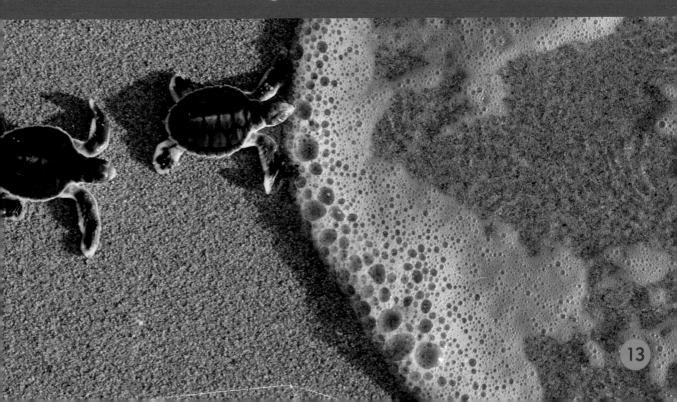

They find the
ocean currents.

They ride them
far out to sea.

The turtles
grow and grow.

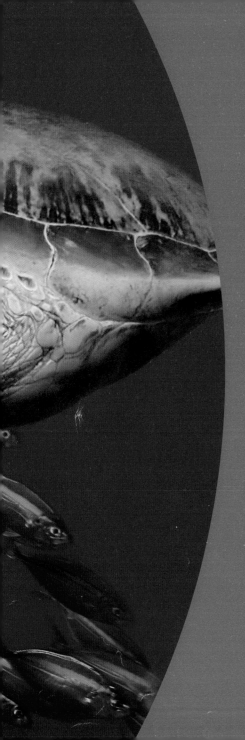

Sea turtles
are good divers.

They dive
to find food.

A loggerhead snaps his strong jaws.

Yum!
A crab makes
a tasty meal!

21

Parts of a Sea Turtle

shell
The hard outer covering that protects a turtle.

front flippers
The two flat front limbs of a sea turtle.

hind flippers
The two flat back limbs of a sea turtle.

Picture Glossary

crab
A type of ocean animal with a hard shell, eight legs, and two claws.

hatchling
A baby turtle that has just cracked open its eggshell.

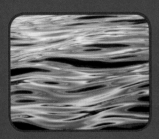

current
Part of the ocean's water that is flowing in a certain direction.

loggerhead
A kind of sea turtle with a very large head and strong jaws.

Index

To Learn More

Learning more is as easy as 1, 2, 3.

1) Go to www.factsurfer.com

2) Enter "sea turtle" into the search box.

3) Click the "Surf" button to see a list of websites.

With factsurfer.com, finding more information is just a click away.